GUITAR STAR IN 30 DAYS

Learning guitar made easy for kids

David Aldridge

David Aldridge
GUITAR SCHOOL

WHAT PARENTS ARE SAYING

"My son has been learning the guitar for a little while and loves it. David explains everything to a level that my child understands."

Shelly Butler

"David's beginner book is an excellent stepping stone to get kids into learning the guitar and keeping it fun. My son has come out of his shell and gained lots of confidence by learning to play the guitar."

Louise Goss

"Archie is learning an outstanding balance of guitar technique and songs, highly recommended,"

Rob Sanderson

WHAT KIDS ARE SAYING

"I can play now, and playing the guitar makes me happy."

Isabella, age 12

"I love my guitar lessons because it's fun and I like learning new songs."

Samuel, age 9

"The lessons are fun, helpful and entertaining. I like learning new songs to play for my family."

Milly-Jey, age 10

This book belongs to...

CONTENTS PAGE

WHY I WROTE THIS BOOK

After 20 years of teaching experience, I was dissatisfied with the supplementary guitar teaching materials out there in the market. I could not find a book that was suitable for our unique style of teaching that out-produced our contemporaries by as much as 95% in helping children achieve their guitar goals above their original expectations. We needed a book that could capture students' attention and motivate them to complete their guitar study, and I simply could not find it.

And thus, Guitar Star In 30 Days was born.

Over time, we noticed that David Aldridge Guitar Students became more determined and confident in themselves and their playing as a result of taking our courses.

The heart of this book comes from our desire to give children a way of expressing their creativity freely and openly through guitar-playing.

It is undoubtedly our hope that you find this book fun, friendly and informative. Each daily lesson is created at the appropriate level for the young, beginner guitarist. By using an incremental approach to lessons, children start with the most basic skills and gradually build up to more advanced ones. We fully support kids learning intentionally!

This book will transform your child into somebody who trusts in their abilities to take on any brand new skill right from the beginning stage.

The lessons I share clearly and actionably will transform your child's confidence. When that happens, you may wish to contact our school and explore us helping you apply this even further.

GUITAR STAR IN 30 DAYS WEBSITE:

Visit Guitar Star In 30 days website and receive your FREE bonus video delivered straight to your inbox.

How To Use The Book

To get the most from the book simply follow the daily steps. Using a combination of a song-based and skilled-based approach, each lesson is pitched at the right level. As you progress through the book, the lessons increase in difficulty. Our goal is to bring a smile to your little one's face as they bask in their sense of accomplishment.

Link for Audio track

Use this think for the audio track where you see this symbol

davidguitarcoach.co.uk/audio-tracks

Our Advice:

Watch the bonus video on top tips to get you started. Practice what you've learned for 5-10 minutes per day. Believe in yourself and transform into a proud Guitar Star!

Want to take the Online Course that accompanies the book?
Visit: davidguitarcoach.co.uk/30-days

Again, to receive the bonus video that comes with this book,
visit: davidguitarcoach.co.uk/bonus-videos
or send an email to:
info@davidguitarcoach.co.uk

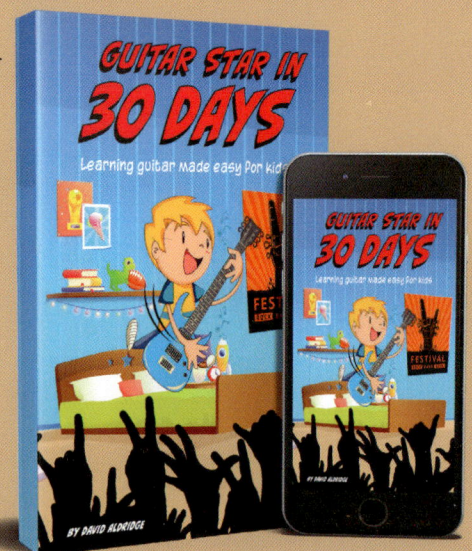

ABOUT THE AUTHOR

Hi, I'm David. I am a passionate and friendly guitar teacher who makes learning guitar fun for kids.

My courses and teaching are known for being very stress-free and engaging. But most importantly, I am known for my incredible skills on how to teach students to play guitar in the most effective and fun way possible.

You will be able to see real progress from my coaching in no time.

Enjoy!

David Aldridge

TOOLS NEEDED TO COMPLETE THE BOOK

Guitar Pick

Electric or acoustic guitar

Stool

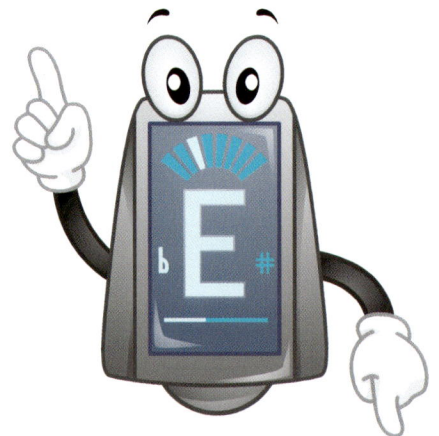

Music stand

Tuner

LESSON 1

IT'S EASY PEASY

DAY 1

Doesn't A Guitar Kinda Look Like A Giraffe?

In today's lesson, you'll get to know all the parts of your guitar.

*Lesson Time, 5 minutes

Did you know?
There are two types of guitars: electric and acoustic ones.

Electric

Acoustic

PARTS OF THE GUITAR

Challenge
Use the diagram below to find all the parts of the guitar, a great way to learn is to test yourself with your guitar without looking at the book. Get a parent to help.

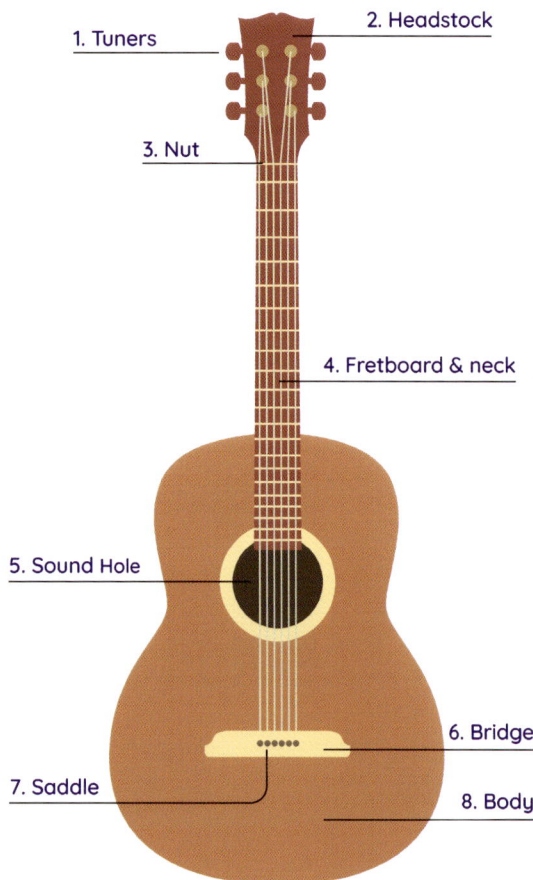

1. Tuners
2. Headstock
3. Nut
4. Fretboard & neck
5. Sound Hole
6. Bridge
7. Saddle
8. Body

Tick the boxes when you can name all the parts of the guitar

Smart Tip.
Have Mum or Dad test you on all the parts on your guitar.

1. Tuners ☐
2. Headstock ☐
3. Nut ☐
4. Fretboard & neck ☐
5. Sound hole ☐
6. Bridge ☐
7. Saddle ☐
8. Body ☐

David Aldridge GUITAR SCHOOL

learn.davidguitarcoach.co.uk/30-days

FUN TIME!

Get your crayons at the ready...

Challenge

Colour in each part of the guitar with the corresponding colour:

Head = **BLUE**
Frets = **GREEN**
Tuners = **RED**
Body = **PURPLE**
Bridge = **ORANGE**

DAY 2
Elephants **A**nd **D**onkeys
Grow **B**ig **E**ars

In today's lesson, you'll get to know the numbers and letters on each string.

*Lesson Time, 5 minutes

Did you know?
A guitar has six strings, and each string has its own letter and number.

Challenge
Use the diagram below to find the following:

1. String: **6, 4** & **2** on your guitar
2. Now find string: **D, A** & **B** on your guitar
3. Memorise: **E**lephants **A**nd **D**onkeys **G**row **B**ig **E**ars

E A D G B E

6 5 4 3 2 1

Smart Tip
Remember, the 'thickest' string is #6, and the 'thinnest' #1. You can use the sentence **E**lephants **A**nd **D**onkeys **G**row **B**ig **E**ars to help you remember the letters and order of each string. You are going from string **6** to **1.**

DAY 3

Let's Tune-Up

In today's lesson, you'll learn how to tune your guitar using a clip-on tuner.

*Lesson Time, 10 minutes

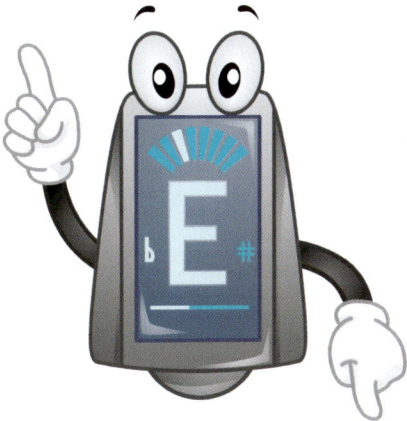

Did you know?
Turning the tuning pegs 'clockwise' makes the pitch higher, and 'anti-clockwise' makes the pitch lower.

Smart Tip
You'll need to know the open strings' names covered in the previous lesson (Day 2).

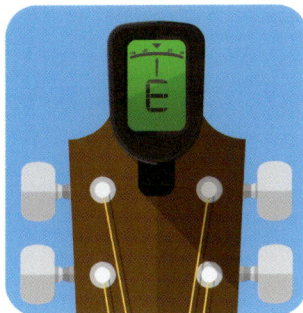

Challenge
1. Clip the tuner onto the end of your guitar
2. Pluck the 6th string (around one pluck per-second) and turn the tuning peg to the correct letter.
3. Follow the steps for each string, making sure to tune each string to the correct letter.

Alternatively, you can also watch a video on how to tune -

www.youtube.com/c/DavidAldridgeGuitarSchools

Remember - Tune your guitar each time you practice.

DAY 4
How To Hold Your Guitar like A POP STAR

In today's lesson, you'll learn how to hold the guitar like the rock/pop star you're going to become.

*Lesson Time, 5 minutes

Did you know?
You can play the guitar in two different ways: sitting down or standing up using a guitar strap.

Challenge
1. Sit with the guitar on your right thigh
2. Your right elbow sits on top of the guitar
3. The right hand is over the soundhole

Smart Tip
Practice sitting with your guitar and perfecting your POP-STAR LOOK!

DAY 5
My Guitar Hands

Today, you'll learn the finger numbers on your left hand.

*Lesson Time, 5 minutes

Remember!
Index - **1st finger**
Middle - **2nd finger**
Ring - **3rd finger**
Pinky - **4th finger**

Challenge
Wiggle each left-hand finger, starting with finger one then two, three and four.

Finger Numbers

4 3 2 1

CHECKLIST & QUIZ

Complete the checklist and have fun with the quiz.

Checklist.

I know all the parts on my guitar. ☐

I know the numbers and letters of each string. ☐

I know how to tune my guitar. ☐

I know how to hold my guitar pick. ☐

I know the numbers of my left-hand fingers. ☐

Quiz Time - Tick the correct answer

How many strings does a guitar have?

100 ☐

10 ☐

4 ☐

6 ☐

What is the letter of each string?

E A D G B E ☐

D D G B A C ☐

A D B G A E ☐

How often should I tune my guitar?

Once a week ☐

Every day ☐

Yearly ☐

How do I hold my guitar?

Behind my head ☐

On my thigh ☐

Balancing on my head ☐

What number is my little finger?

1 ☐

3 ☐

2 ☐

4 ☐

CONGRATULATIONS!

You've completed all the work for LESSON 1.

LESSON 2

LEMON SQUEEZY

DAY 6
Holding A Guitar Pick

In today's lesson, you'll learn how to hold a guitar pick.

*Lesson Time, 5 minutes

Did you know?
A guitar pick can also be called a plectrum, and plectrums can come in different thicknesses.

Challenge
Learn how to hold your guitar pick by following the diagram and instructions below.

1. Hold the pick in your right hand between your thumb and outer edge of your index finger
2. Point the tip of the guitar pick towards your guitar strings and soundhole
3. Practice holding your guitar pick a few time each day

Smart Tip
Holding the pick close to the pointy bit will help you gain control when you're plucking each string.

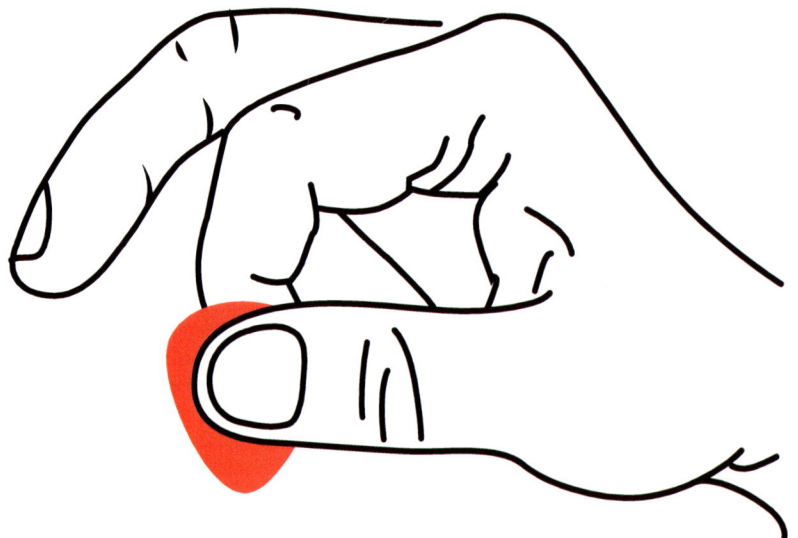

DAY 7
How To Pluck The Strings

In today's lesson, you'll learn how to pluck the guitar strings using a pick.

*Lesson Time, 5 minutes

Did you know?
Picking is one of the most essential skills in guitar playing. You're creating the sound of each note when you pluck.

Challenge
Use the diagram and instructions below to help you learn how to pluck each string correctly.

1. Hold the pick between your thumb and forefinger
2. Start at the 6th string and practice down picks, SLOWLY!
3. Tick the boxes on the next page when you've completed eight down plucks on each string.

PICK ON STRING

David Aldridge

Front of pick touching string

DOWN PICK

David Aldridge

Pick moves down through the string

I have completed:

8 down plucks on the 6th string	☐
8 down plucks on the 5th string	☐
8 down plucks on the 4th string	☐
8 down plucks on the 3rd string	☐
8 down plucks on the 2nd string	☐
8 down plucks on the 1st string	☐

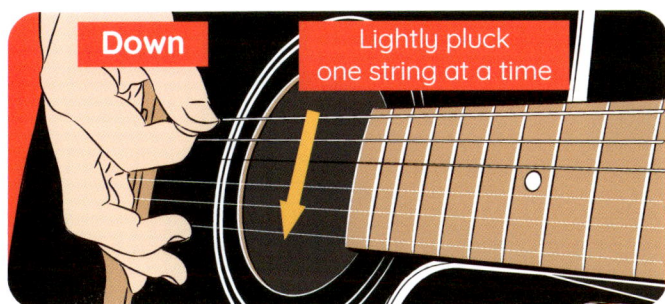

Down

Lightly pluck one string at a time

Smart Tip
Practice picking daily for 5 minutes. Use picking as a warm-up exercise before you play anything else!

David Aldridge
GUITAR SCHOOL

DAY 8
How To Strum

In today's lesson, you'll learn how to strum your guitar. Knowing how to strum makes you a guitar star.

*Lesson Time, 10 minutes

Challenge

Learn how to strum your guitar like a POP STAR. Remember to use the diagram and instructions below.

1. Hold the pick in between your thumb and forefinger (day 6).
2. Start at the 6th string, and strum 'lightly' from string 6 to 1, gliding over each string downwards towards the floor (down).
3. Keep on practicing, and when you can strum all six strings easily, move onto the LITTLE ROCK STAR CHALLENGE on the next page.

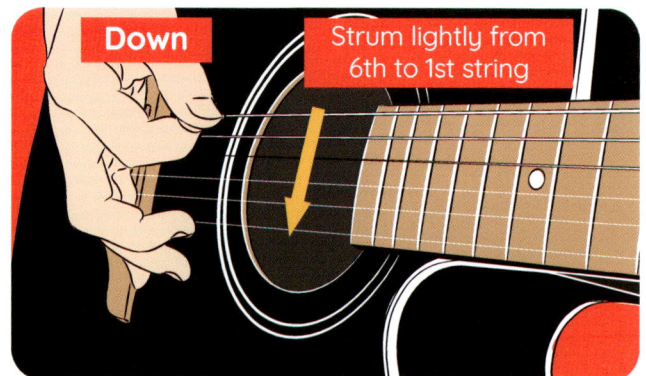

Down — Strum lightly from 6th to 1st string

Smart Tip

When strumming your guitar, 'blend' the sound of all the strings together creating one sound.

LITTLE ROCK STAR CHALLENGE!

Are you ready? Practice strumming the lessons 1-4, with 8 strums on each "exercise."

*Tick the boxes once you have completed the challenge

Strum from string 6 -> 1 ☐

Strum from string 5 -> 1 ☐

Strum from string 4 -> 1 ☐

Strum from string 3 -> 1 ☐

WELL DONE ON COMPLETING LITTLE ROCK STAR CHALLENGE!

DAY 9
Where to place your fingers

In today's lesson, Learn how to read chord boxes and to place your fingers on the fretboard for playing chords. Follow the diagrams and instructions below to help you.

*Lesson Time, 10 minutes

Challenge

Learn how to read chord boxes and to place your fingers on the fretboard for playing chords. Follow the diagrams and instructions below to help you.

Every chord has a 'letter' name and sometimes can have a number too, for example, 'G7'.

1. The name is always at the top of the chord box (step 1)
2. Hold your guitar in the correct position. Now find strings 6 -> 1 and then frets 1,2 & 3. (step 2)
3. Place your 3rd finger on string 1 at the 3rd fret. You now have a chord of 'G'. (step 3)

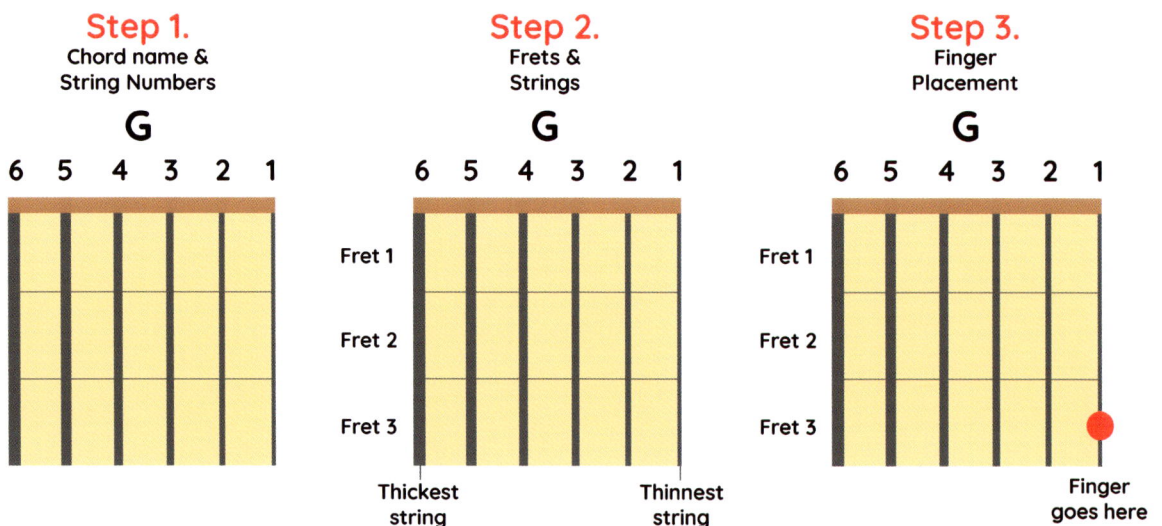

Step 1.
Chord name &
String Numbers

G

6 5 4 3 2 1

Step 2.
Frets &
Strings

G

6 5 4 3 2 1

Fret 1

Fret 2

Fret 3

Thickest string   Thinnest string

Step 3.
Finger
Placement

G

6 5 4 3 2 1

Fret 1

Fret 2

Fret 3

Finger goes here

Smart Tip
Placing a mirror in front of you helps you to see your fingers when finding the chords.

DAY 10
How to Play Chords

In today's lesson, you'll learn how to play one-finger chords, G,G7 & Em. Then, you'll learn to play your first SONG, the 'Blending Song'

*Lesson Time, 15 minutes

Did you know?
We use chords to play along with singers. Follow the diagram and instructions below to help you learn some cool chords.

Challenge
Become a star at playing chords. Use the diagram and instructions below and on the following page to help you learn some cool chords. (Follow diagram)

1. Place the pad of your thumb on the back of the guitar neck (Follow diagram)
2. When playing G and G7, use your fingertip to push the string down to the fretboard, and make sure you keep the string pushed down as you strum.
3. Practice changing between G - G7 & Em, with four down strums on each chord. (How to strum is covered in Day 8)

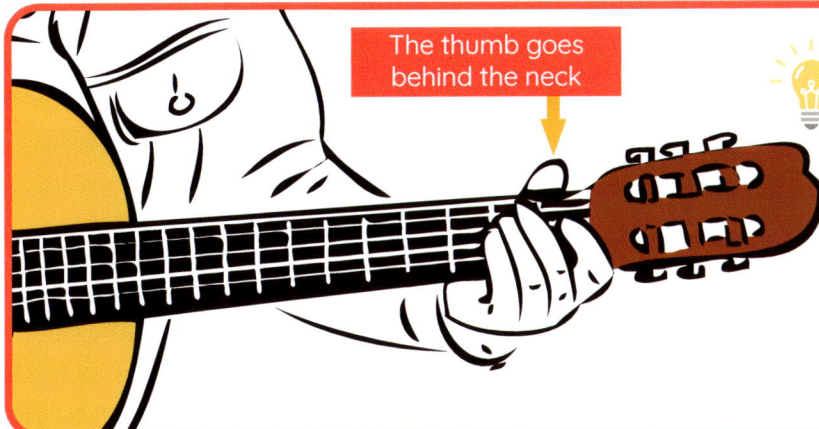

The thumb goes behind the neck

Smart Tip
If you're getting a 'buzzing' sound from the chord, add more pressure by pushing more into the string; also, play next to the fret the metal strip, but not on the strip.

Em
Open Strings

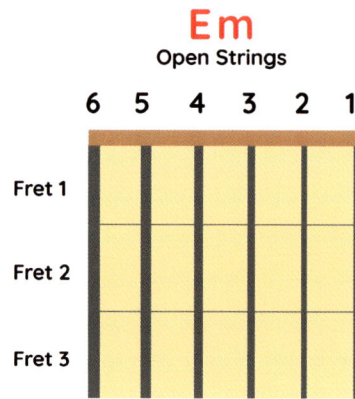

Practice 4 down strums on Em, strumming only from the 3rd string

G7

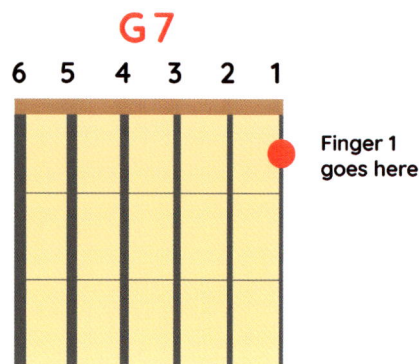

Finger 1
goes here

Practice 4 down strums on 'G7'

G

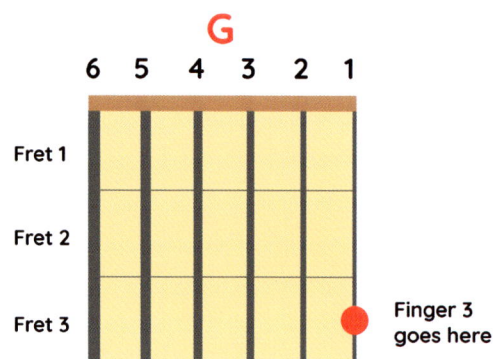

Finger 3
goes here

Practice 4 down strums on 'G'

THE BLENDING SONG

Blend the sound like fruit in a blender,
all mushy and colourful

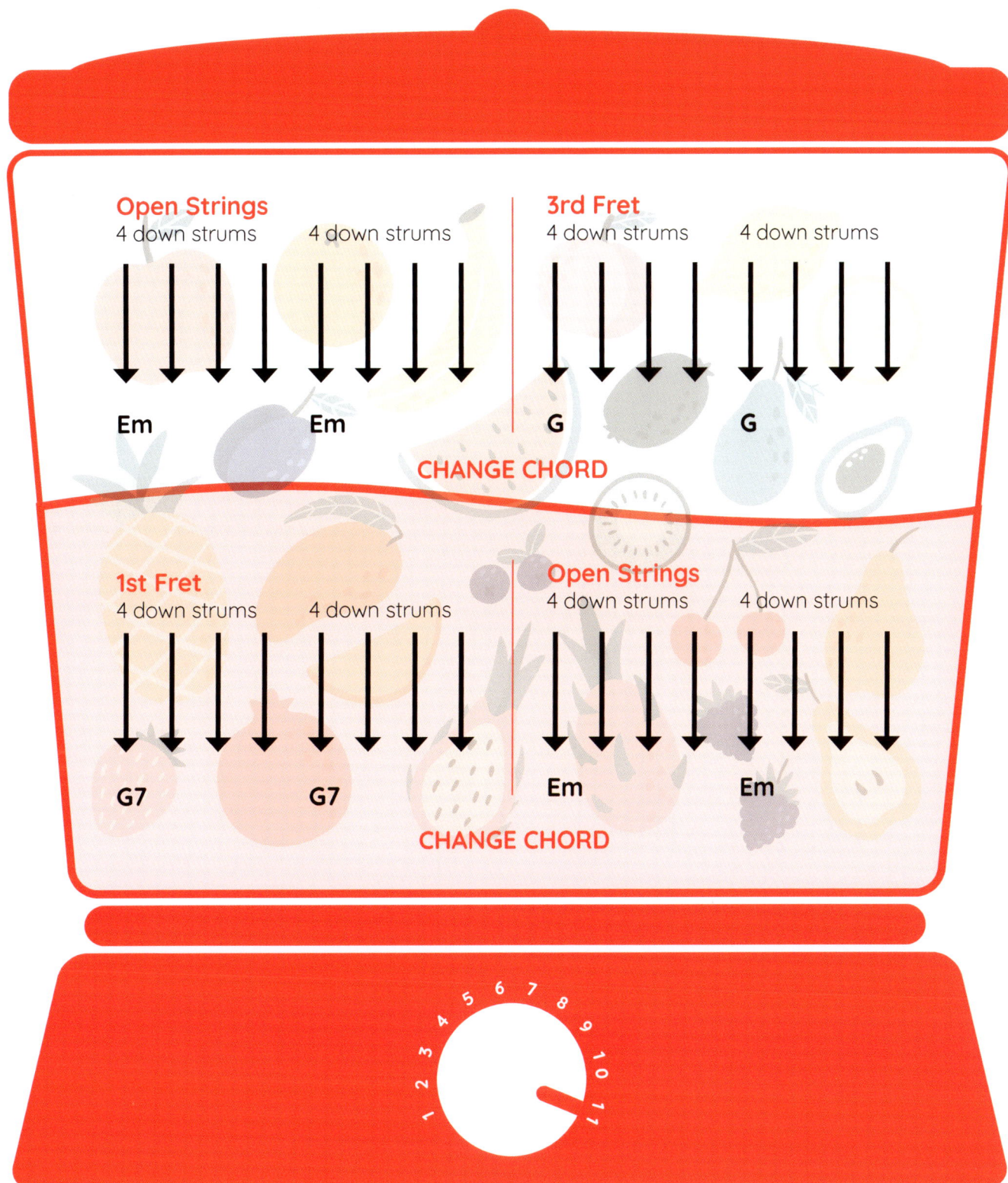

Open Strings
4 down strums   4 down strums

Em   Em

3rd Fret
4 down strums   4 down strums

G   G

CHANGE CHORD

1st Fret
4 down strums   4 down strums

G7   G7

Open Strings
4 down strums   4 down strums

Em   Em

CHANGE CHORD

David Aldridge GUITAR SCHOOL

Fun guitar fact:
The first guitar was created in ancient Egypt.

CONGRATULATIONS ON COMPLETING LESSON 2.

You're well on your way to becoming a Guitar Star!

MY PRACTICE LIST

1. Practice picking each day
2. Practice strumming each day
3. Practice the blending song

I'VE GOT THIS!

David Aldridge GUITAR SCHOOL

CHECKLIST & QUIZ

Complete the checklist and have fun with the quiz.

Checklist.

I know how to hold my guitar pick? ☐

Can I pluck down each string? ☐

I know how to strum my guitar? ☐

Can I play Em, G & G7 chords? ☐

Can I play the Blending Song? ☐

Quiz Time - Tick the correct answer

I'm holding the pick with?

Pinky and thumb` ☐

Index and thumb ☐

How many plucks to do on each string, daily?

40 ☐

8 ☐

100 ☐

Which direction should I strum?

Down to floor ☐

Up to the sky ☐

Sideways ☐

Which part of the finger do you use when playing chords?

Nail ☐

Fingertip ☐

Knuckle ☐

How many down strums should I practice on each chord?

1 ☐

3 ☐

2 ☐

4 ☐

CONGRATULATIONS!

You've completed all the work for LESSON 1.

LESSON 3

BELIEVE IN YOURSELF

DAY 11
How To Play Arpeggios

today's lesson, you'll learn how
to play arpeggios.

*Lesson Time, 10 minutes

Did you know?
Arpeggio is an Italian word, which means 'To play the Harp'.

Challenge

Learn how to pluck an Em arpeggio pattern using strings 1, 2 & 3.
See the diagram below to help you.

1. Hold the pick in your right hand between your thumb and the outer edge of your index finger
2. Point the tip of the guitar pick towards your guitar strings and soundhole Pluck strings **3** -> **2** -> **1** -> **2**. Repeat the pattern four times.

E minor arpeggio

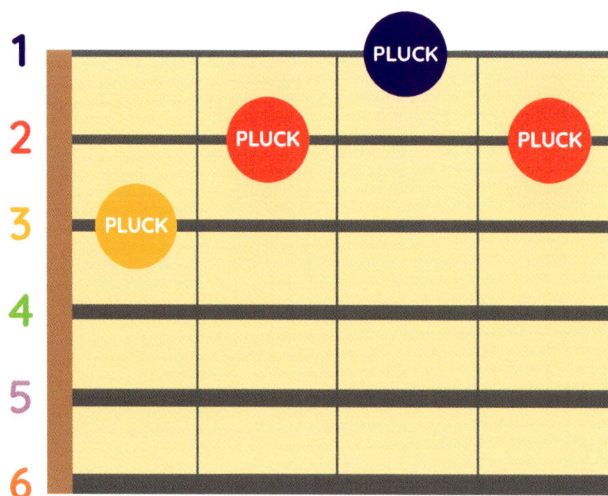

Smart Tip
Arpeggios are broken chords where the notes are plucked separately, unlike chords where the notes sound simultaneously by strumming.

DAY 12
How To Read Tabs

In today's lesson, you'll learn how to read tabs. They tell you where to place your fingers on the guitar's fretboard.

*Lesson Time, 10 minutes

Challenge

Play frets 1, 2 & 3 on the first string using the diagram below.

1. Find string 1 on the tab below
2. Find frets 1, 2 & 3 on the first string of your guitar
3. Now play the notes separately

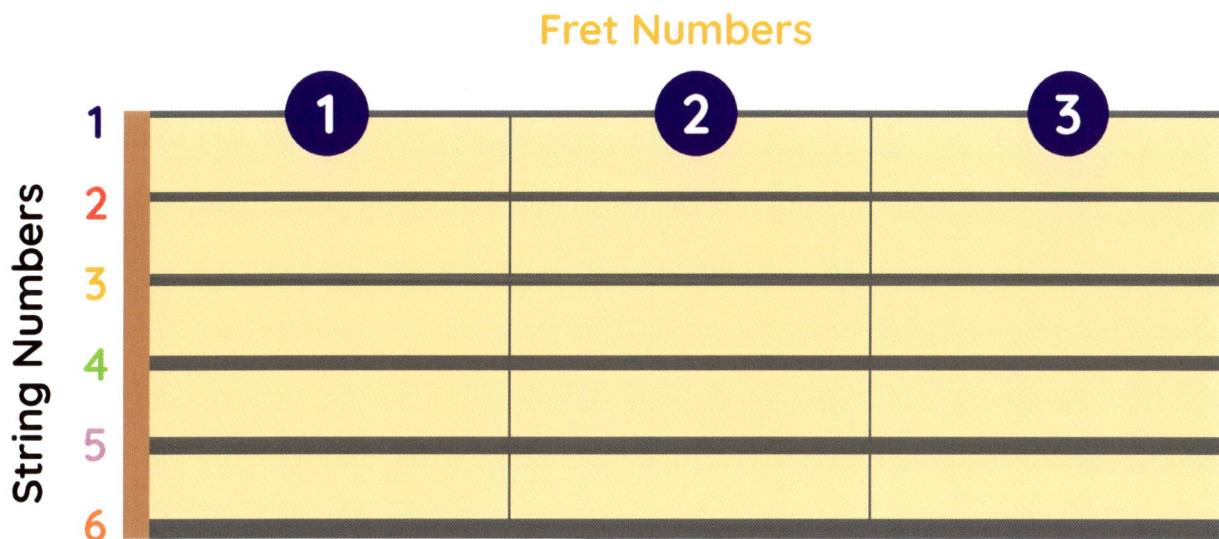

Fret Numbers

String Numbers

1
2
3
4
5
6

Smart Tip
The circled numbers are the frets you play on the strings.

DAY 13
The Harp Song

In today's lesson, you'll learn how to play "The Harp Song" using the arpeggio pattern from Day 11.

*Lesson Time, 20 minutes

Challenge

Using the chords of Em, G and G7, you'll learn how to play "The Harp Song".

1. Use your guitar pick for plucking the strings
2. Follow the chord pattern **Em** -> **G7** -> **G** -> **Em**
3. Pluck the string pattern **3** -> **2** -> **1** -> **2** on each chord

The Harp Song

DAY 14
How To Play The G Scale

In today's lesson, you'll learn how to play the G scale. The notes in scales make melodies in songs.

*Lesson Time, 10 minutes

Did you know?
Scales can go forwards, 'ascending', meaning the notes get higher in pitch, and backwards, 'descending', the notes get lower in pitch.

Challenge
Learn how to play the G scale using the diagram below.

1. Use your guitar pick for plucking the strings
2. Make sure your finger is pushing the string down entirely for the note to sound clear.
3. Go slowly, and play ascending (up) and then descending (down)

The G Scale Ascending

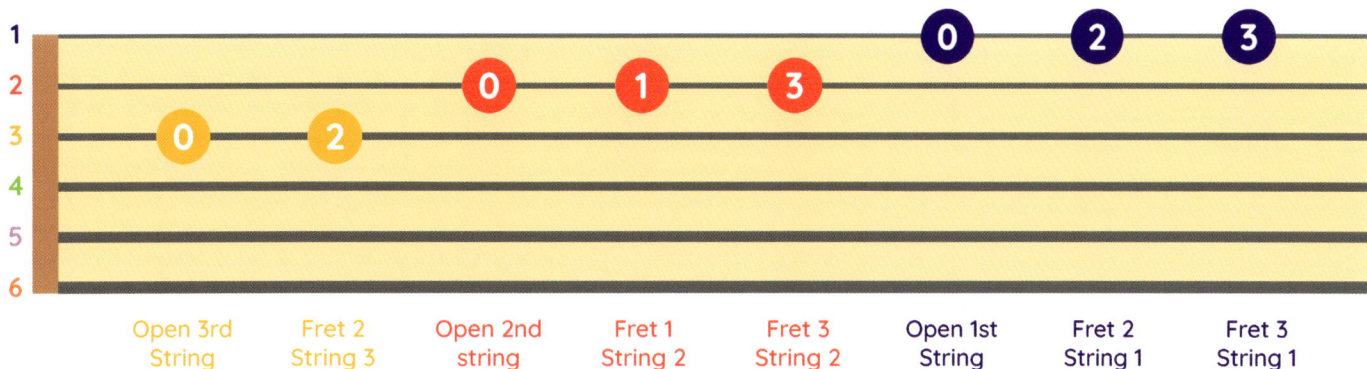

| Open 3rd String | Fret 2 String 3 | Open 2nd string | Fret 1 String 2 | Fret 3 String 2 | Open 1st String | Fret 2 String 1 | Fret 3 String 1 |

The G Scale Descending

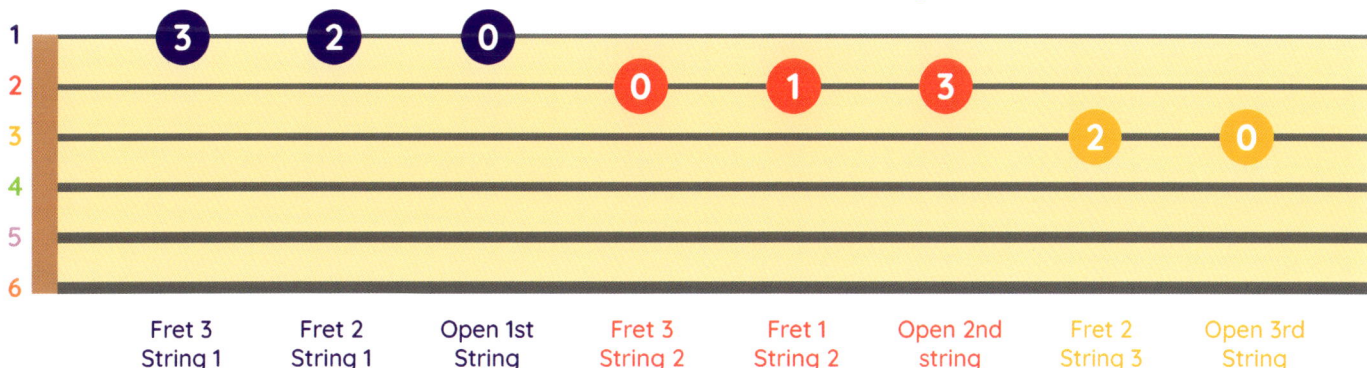

| Fret 3 String 1 | Fret 2 String 1 | Open 1st String | Fret 3 String 2 | Fret 1 String 2 | Open 2nd string | Fret 2 String 3 | Open 3rd String |

Smart Tip
Practicing the G scale will help you learn how to play songs quickly.

DAY 15 🎧 TRACK 2
Incy Wincy Spider

In today's lesson, you'll learn how to play "Incy Wincy Spider" using notes from the G scale.

*Lesson Time, 20 minutes

Challenge
Learn to play "Incy Wincy Spider" and impress your friends and family.

1. Sing and clap the rhythm before learning the notes
2. Learn and play all the notes.
3. Play through the whole song from start to finish.

Incy Wincy Spider

In -	cy	win -	cy	spi -	der	went	up	the	wa -	ter	spout
down	came	the	rain	and	washed	the	spi-	der	out		
out	came	the	sun	and	dried	up	all	the	rain		
in-	cy	win-	cy	spi-	der	climbed	up	the	spout	a-	gain

Smart Tip
Play through the whole song 3 times each day to help you speed up and play smoothly and accurately.

CHECKLIST & QUIZ

Complete the checklist and have fun with the quiz.

Checklist.

I know how to play arpeggios. ☐
Can I play the "Harp Song" ☐
I know how to read tabs ☐
I know how to play the G scale. ☐
Can I play "Incy Wincy Spider" ☐

Quiz Time - Tick the correct answer

Arpeggios are chords plucked out?
True ☐
False ☐

"The Harp Song" uses the same arpeggio picking pattern on each chord.
True ☐
False ☐

Tabs are used to tune your guitar.
True ☐
False ☐

The G scale uses all 6 strings?
True ☐
False ☐

'Incy Wincy Spider' uses all the notes from the G Scale?
True ☐
False ☐

Congratulations!

You've completed all the work for LESSON 3.

David Aldridge
GUITAR SCHOOL

Double decker bus height 4.38 metres high

GUITA

LESSON 4

YOU ARE TALENTED

DAY 16
Coffee & Tea

In today's lesson, you'll have fun learning how to strum basic patterns. We'll be using the words 'COFFEE' and 'TEA' to help with rhythm.

*Lesson Time, 10 minutes

Challenge

To strum 4 easy patterns using combinations of down and up strums.

1. Remember to hold the pick in your right hand between your thumb and the outer edge of your index finger.
2. We use the word 'TEA' (one syllable) for down strumming, and 'COF-FEE' (two syllables) for DOWN and UP. (see diagram below)
3. Now have fun completing the 4 strumming patterns on the next page. Make sure to practice them four times each.

CO-FFEE

Down & up strum

TEA

Down strum

💡 **Smart Tip**
Clap the rhythm and say the words before strumming the patterns.

COFFEE & TEA

1. ↓ ↑   ↓   ↓   ↓
COF - FEE   TEA   TEA   TEA

2. ↓   ↓ ↑   ↓   ↓
TEA   COF - FEE   TEA   TEA

3. ↓   ↓   ↓ ↑   ↓
TEA   TEA   COF - FEE   TEA

4. ↓   ↓   ↓   ↓ ↑
TEA   TEA   TEA   COF - FEE

David Aldridge GUITAR SCHOOL

DAY 17
Chocolate & Tea

In today's lesson, you'll have fun learning how to strum a few more basic patterns. We'll be using the words CHOCOLATE and TEA to help with rhythm.

*Lesson Time, 10 minutes

Challenge
To strum basic patterns using words cho-co-late and tea.

1. Remember to hold the pick in your right hand between your thumb and the outer edge of your index finger.
2. We use the word 'TEA' (one syllable) for down strumming and 'CHO-CO-LATE' for DOWN - UP - DOWN (three syllables).
3. Have fun completing the strumming patterns on the next page. Make sure to practice them four times each.

TEA

↓

Down & up strum

CHO-CO-LATE

↓ ↑ ↓

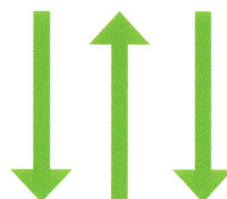

Down & up down strum

Did you know?
Most pop and rock songs use combinations of DOWN and UP strumming patterns.

CHOCOLATE & TEA

1.

↓ ↑ ↓   ↓   ↓   ↓

CHO-CO-LATE   TEA   TEA   TEA

2.

↓   ↓ ↑ ↓   ↓   ↓

TEA   CHO-CO-LATE   TEA   TEA

3.

↓   ↓   ↓ ↑ ↓   ↓

TEA   TEA   CHO-CO-LATE   TEA

4.

↓   ↓   ↓   ↓ ↑ ↓

TEA   TEA   TEA   CHO-CO-LATE

DAY 18
Coca-cola & Tea

In today's lesson, you'll have fun learning more strumming patterns. We'll be using the words 'TEA' and 'COCA-COLA' to help with rhythm.

*Lesson Time, 10 minutes

Challenge

To strum rhythm patterns using the words Co-ca-co-la and tea.

1. Hold the pick in your right hand between your thumb and the outer edge of your index finger.
2. Use the word 'TEA' (one syllable) for down strumming and 'COCA-COLA' (four syllables) for DOWN - UP - DOWN - UP.
3. Have fun completing the strumming patterns on the next page. Make sure to practice them four times each.

TEA

Down strum

CO-CA-CO-LA

Down up down up strum

💡 **Smart Tip**
Make sure you're strumming all 6 strings evenly.

COCACOLA & TEA

1. ↓ ↑ ↓ ↑   ↓   ↓   ↓

CO-CA-CO-LA   TEA   TEA   TEA

2. ↓   ↓ ↑ ↓ ↑   ↓   ↓

TEA   CO-CA-CO-LA   TEA   TEA

3. ↓   ↓   ↓ ↑ ↓ ↑   ↓

TEA   TEA   CO-CA-CO-LA   TEA

4. ↓   ↓   ↓   ↓ ↑ ↓ ↑

TEA   TEA   TEA   CO-CA-CO-LA

DAY 19
Tea, Coffee, Chocolate & Coca-cola

In today's lesson, you'll strum all of the combinations of TEA, COFFEE, CHOCOLATE and COCA-COLA that you just learned.

*Lesson Time, 10 minutes

Challenge

To strum all of the rhythmic patterns using down and up strums from days 16-18.

1. Hold the pick in your right hand between your thumb and the outer edge of your index finger.
2. Remember, 'TEA' down strum. 'COF-FEE' down-up. 'CHO-CO-LATE' down-up-down. 'CO-CA-CO-LA' down-up-down-up.
3. Have fun playing all the different combinations of strumming patterns.

TEA

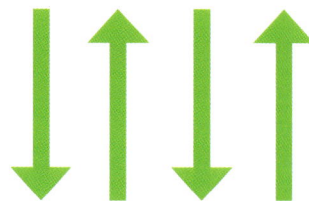

Down strum

CO-CA-CO-LA

Down up down up strum

CHO-CO-LATE

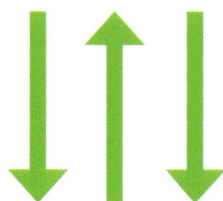

Down & up down strum

CO-FFEE

Down & up strum

COMBINATIONS

1. ↓ ↑ ↓ ↑   ↓   ↓ ↑   ↓

CO-CA-CO-LA   TEA   COF - FEE   TEA

2. ↓   ↓ ↑ ↓   ↓   ↓ ↑

TEA   CHO-CO-LATE   TEA   COF - FEE

3. ↓   ↓   ↓ ↑ ↓ ↑   ↓

TEA   TEA   CO-CA-CO-LA   TEA

4. ↓   ↓ ↑ ↓   ↓ ↓ ↑ ↓ ↑

TEA   CHO-CO-LATE   TEA   CO-CA-CO-LA

DAY 20
The Thirsty Song

In today's lesson, you'll learn how to play a fun little song to practice all the strumming patterns called 'The Thirsty Song'.

*Lesson Time, 10 minutes

Challenge

You are playing 'The Thirsty Song' from start to finish.

1. Clap 'The Thirsty Song' from start to finish using the words to help with the rhythm.
2. Strum evenly as you play through the song.
3. Complete the checklist for lesson 4.

💡 Smart Tip
We read music from left to right just like reading a book.

THE THIRSTY SONG

1. ↓ ↑ ↓ ↑   ↓   ↓   ↓ ↑

2. ↓ ↓   ↓ ↑   ↓ ↓

3. ↓ ↑ ↓   ↓   ↓ ↑   ↓

4. ↓ ↑ ↓ ↑   ↓ ↑ ↓   ↓   ↓

CHECKLIST & QUIZ
Complete the list and quiz.

Checklist.

Can I now strum TEA (crotchet) ☐

Can I now strum COFFEE (quaver) ☐

Can I now strum CHOCOLATE (triplet) ☐

Can I now strum COCA-COLA (semiquaver) ☐

Can I play The Thirsty Song ☐

Congratulations!
You've completed all the work for LESSON 4.

You can now strum lots of different patterns that are used in rock and pop songs.

LESSON 5

FUN AND EASY SONGS

DAY 21 🎧 TRACK 3
Twinkle, Twinkle, Little Star

In today's lesson, you'll learn how to play Twinkle, Twinkle, Little Star.

*Lesson Time, 10 minutes

Steps

1. Listen to the audio track of Twinkle, Twinkle, Little Star provided with the book as a digital download.
2. Before playing, sing and clap the song to help with the tune and rhythm.
3. Now play the music from start to finish on your guitar.

Twinkle, Twinkle, Little Star

Twin - kle, Twin - kle, Lit - tle Star, How I Won - der What - You Are

Up - Abo - ove - The, World So High Like A Dia - mond In The Sky

Twin - kle, Twin - kle, Lit - tle Star, How I Won - der What - You Are

💡 **Smart Tip**
Remember to go slow!! Speed will come with practice.

DAY 22 🎧 TRACK 4

The Wheels On The Bus

In today's lesson, you'll learn how to play The Wheels On The Bus.

*Lesson Time, 10 minutes

Steps

1. Listen to the audio track of The Wheels On The Bus provided with the book as a digital download.
2. Before playing, sing and clap the song to help with the tune and rhythm.
3. Now play the music from start to finish on your guitar.

The Wheels On The Bus

| The | wheels | on | the | bus | go | Round | and | round | round | and | round |

| Round | and | round, | the | wheels | on | the | bus | go | round | and | round |

| all | day | long |

💡 Smart Tip

Remember to hold the pick in your right hand between your thumb and the outer edge of your index finger.

David Aldridge GUITAR SCHOOL

DAY 23 🎧 TRACK 5
Row, Row, Your Boat

In today's lesson, you'll learn how to play Row, Row, Row Your Boat.

*Lesson Time, 10 minutes

Steps

1. Listen to the audio track of Row, Row, Row Your Boat provided with the book as a digital download.
2. Before playing, sing and clap the song to help with the tune and rhythm.
3. Now play the music from start to finish on your guitar.

Row, Row, Row Your Boat

| Row, | row, | row | your | boat | Gent | -ly | down | the | stream |

| me- | ri- | ly, | me- | ri- | ly, | me- | ri- | ly, | me- | ri- | ly, |

| life | is | but | a | dream |

💡 Smart Tip
Remember to use the correct fingers on your left hand.
Use finger 1, for the 1st fret, finger 2 - 2nd fret, and finger 3 - 3rd fret.

DAY 24

Rain, Rain, Go Away

In today's lesson, you'll learn how to play Rain, Rain, Go Away.

*Lesson Time, 10 minutes

Steps

1. Personalise the song by writing your name on line 2, after the word 'little'
2. Before playing, sing and clap the song to help with the tune and rhythm.
3. Now play the song from start to finish on your guitar.

Rain, Rain, Go Away

3	0	3	3	0	3	3	0	5	3	3	0
Rain,	rain	go	a-	way	Come	a-	gain	some	o-	ther	day,

1	1	3	3	1	1	3	3	0	0	1	1
Lit-	tle			wants	to	play	Rain,	rain	go	a-	way

Smart Tip

By playing Rain, Rain, Go Away many times helps you to speed up the notes!

learn.davidguitarcoach.co.uk/30-days

DAY 25
Baa, Baa, Black Sheep

In today's lesson, you'll learn how to play Baa, Baa, Black Sheep.

*Lesson Time, 10 minutes

Steps

1. Listen to the audio track of Baa, Baa, Black Sheep provided with the book as a digital download.
2. Before playing, sing and clap the song to help with the tune and rhythm.
3. Now play the song from start to finish on your guitar.

Baa, Baa, Black Sheep

Baa baa black sheep, have you an- y wool? yes sir, yes sir,

three bags full One for the ma- ster, one for the dame

one for the lit- tle boy who lives down the lane Baa baa black sheep, have you an- y wool?

yes sir, yes sir, three bags full

Smart Tip
Play Baa, Baa, Black Sheep three times all the way through. You'll notice the notes getting faster!

CHECKLIST

Complete the checklist.

Checklist.

Can I play Twinkle, Twinkle, Little Star? ☐

Can I play The Wheels On The Bus? ☐

Can I play Row, Row, Row Your Boat? ☐

Can I play Rain, Rain, Go Away? ☐

Can I play Baa, Baa, Black Sheep? ☐

David Aldridge GUITAR SCHOOL

Fun guitar fact:
A man once married his guitar.

Just Married

LESSON 6

TAKE ME TO THE STAGE

DAY 26
Ode To Joy

TRACK 8

In today's lesson, you'll learn how to play Ode To Joy.

*Lesson Time, 10 minutes

Steps
1. Listen to the audio track of Ode To Joy provided with the book as a digital download.
2. Before playing, sing and clap the song to help with the tune and rhythm.
3. Now play the music from start to finish on your guitar.

Ode To Joy

Smart Tip
Start slow, making sure you're using the correct fingers.

DAY 27
TRACK 9

Hot Cross Buns

In today's lesson, you'll learn how to play Hot Cross Buns.

*Lesson Time, 10 minutes

Steps

1. Listen to the audio track of Hot Cross Buns provided with the book as a digital download.
2. Before playing, sing and clap the song to help with the tune and rhythm.
3. Now play the music from start to finish on your guitar.

Hot Cross Buns

Hot   cross   buns!   Hot   cross   buns!

One   a   pen-   ny,   two   a   pen-   ny,   Hot   cross   buns!

Smart Tip
Playing Hot Cross Buns three times in one practice session helps to find the notes quickly!

DAY 28 🎧
Jingle Bells

In today's lesson, you'll learn how to play Jingle Bells.

*Lesson Time, 10 minutes

Steps
1. Listen to the audio track of Jingle Bells provided with the book as a digital download.
2. Before playing, sing and clap the song to help with the tune and rhythm.
3. Now play the music from start to finish on your guitar.

Jingle Bells

Jin- gle bells, Jin- gle bells, Jin- gle all the way

Oh what fun it is to ride in a One horse op- en sleigh!

Jin- gle bells, Jin- gle bells, Jin- gle all the way

Oh what fun it is to ride in a One horse op- en sleigh!

💡 Smart Tip
Try Playing Jingle Bells without looking back at your fingers.

DAY 29 🎧 TRACK 11

Old MacDonald

In today's lesson, you'll learn how to play Old MacDonald Had A Farm.

*Lesson Time, 10 minutes

Steps

1. Listen to the audio track of Old MacDonald provided with the book as a digital download.
2. Before playing, sing and clap the song to help with the tune and rhythm.
3. Now play the music from start to finish on your guitar.

Old MacDonald

Old Mac Don- ald had a farm, E- I- E- I- O

And on that farm he had a pig E- I- E- I- O with an

oink oink here and an oink oink there here an oink, there an oink

ev- erywhere an oink oink Old Mac Don- ald had a farm,

E- I- E- I- O

💡 Smart Tip

Have Mum or Dad sing along as you play Old MacDonald.

DAY 30
Star Performance

In today's lesson, you'll play and perform three songs for family and friends.

*Lesson Time, 10 minutes

Steps

1. Choose three songs from the list below to perform.
2. Remember to face your audience when playing the songs.
3. Take a well-deserved bow after your performance. Congratulations!

Twinkle, Twinkle, Little Star

The Wheels On The Bus

Row, Row, Your Boat

Rain, Rain, Go Away

Baa, Baa, Black Sheep

Ode To Joy

Hot Cross Buns

Jingle Bells

Old McDonald

COMPLETION CERTIFICATE

GUITAR STAR

Well done on completing Guitar Star In 30 Days.
I'm happy to be your teacher and guide you to play all
these fun songs and skills.

Add your name to the certificate, frame it and put
it on the wall for everyone to see!

You are now a Guitar Star!!

If you prefer a digital version of the
certificate sent straight to your inbox
visit:www.davidguitarcoach/my-certificate

Share your child's success on
the David Aldridge Guitar Schools
Facebook community fan page.
Visit: @davidguitarcoach

David Aldridge

David Aldridge
Head Guitar Coach

David Aldridge
GUITAR SCHOOL

QUIZ ANSWERS

LESSON 1

- How many strings does a guitar have? **The correct answer is 6.**
- What is the letter name of each string? **The correct answer is EADGBE.**
- How often should I tune my guitar? **The correct answer is every day.**
- How do I hold my guitar? **The correct answer is on my thigh.**
- What number is my little finger? **The correct answer is number 4.**

LESSON 2

- I'm holding the pick with? **The correct answer is index and thumb.**
- How many pluck to do on each string, daily? **The correct answer is 8.**
- Which direction should I strum? **The correct answer is down to the floor.**
- Which part of the finger do you use when playing chords?
  The correct answer is a fingertip.
- How many down strums should I practice on each chord? **The correct answer is 4.**

LESSON 3

- Arpeggios are chords plucked out? **The correct answer is true.**
- "The Harp Song" uses the same arpeggio picking pattern on each chord?
  The correct answer is true.
- Are tabs used to tune your guitar? **The correct answer is false.**
- Does the G scale uses all 6 strings? **The correct answer is false.**
- "Incy Wincy Spider" uses all the notes from the G scale?
  The correct answer is true.